THOU

THOU

Aisha Sasha John

BookThug · 2014

The production of this book was made possible through the generous assistance of the Canada Council for the Arts and the Ontario Arts Council.

LIBRARY AND ARCHIVES CANADA CATALOGUING IN PUBLICATION

John, Aisha Sasha, author
        Thou / Aisha Sasha John.

Poems.
Issued in print and electronic formats.
ISBN 978-1-77166-033-4 (PBK.).–ISBN 978-1-77166-040-2 (PDF)

        I. Title.

PS8619.O444T46 2014   C811'.6   C2013-908727-3
                                    C2013-908728-1

PRINTED IN CANADA

The Beloved

One went to the door of the Beloved and knocked.
A voice asked: 'Who is there?' He answered: 'It is I.'
The voice said: 'There is no room here for me and thee.'
The door was shut.

After a year of solitude and deprivation
this man returned to the door of the Beloved.
He knocked.
A voice from within asked: 'Who is there?'
The man said: 'It is Thou.'
The door was opened for him.
— Rumi

Contents

Physical.

I arrived here on Saturday.

And today it is Monday.
I don't understand the skies.

They're red —

Yanni I love them
but I do not
know.

All of the baby lambs. All of the cows. (No cows.)

I don't want to be outside. I hate love.

> And
> swollen.

Today a jinn sat beside me at breakfast.

I get three wishes.

A jinn sat to my left at breakfast.
I composed three wishes
in a WordPad document
standing.

The third was about listening

to
my spirit, yours;
the universe, the animals therein,
the stars, events and wind;
to the sun, to waters and steam,
to the tightness at my right hip, my supple neck,
to the waves and the recordings,
to the call to prayer
above the walk from the resto,
to the sadnesses before me,
the inquietude before me, the weakness, the effort I see and the
industry I've met,
to the attempts to gather my attention and to
shun me

and to delight me.

A French woman living in Casablanca

a journalist with too much bronzer
asked if I was from the United States.
No,
I said.

A wave of weakness after I ate the salad.

In French I said to the head waiter I would wait for the others.
Minutes later I returned, and in English said
I changed my mind.
D'accord,
and read two Mrabet stories.
They were brutal.
I was satisfied.

I slept.
A small deft woman pushed her
feet against my tailbone and rubbed
a tonic, an oil, along my back and everywhere.
When she kneaded my right quadricep,
it was physical.

I ate a salad with squares of white cheese.
Passion fruit orange Greek yogurt.
Meanwhile,
it was being suggested
the translators
ate too much at breakfast.

I was a rolling pin, ass raised,
side to side along the
dough of my bed.
The bug which had
forced out my lamb dish the night prior
remained,
attacking my kidneys.
This was my
first experience of my kidneys:
it was physical.

The director. He prescribed
a Thai yoga tonic massage –
for the following morning.
In my wishes I said if.
In my wishes I said if I am with this pain
12 hours from now God –
I will need a massage from God.

Anyway.
Before all that I was okay I thought.
I saw your pit stain in the resto at lunch.
I said, Nice to see you – forcefully.

I barfed the little bit of vervain tea
she advised me not to drink.

I barfed with violence
the supper of lamb
and egg
and bread.
Later, at lunch,
I said with great rehearsal,
It was good, hier soir,
I purged my fear and strategy.

Immediately prior
I had ingested some medicines
the Italian woman gave me.
She said they were for spasms.
Okay.
I had was having spasms.
So I ate them
and
vomited on the bottom bed corner.
And then later into the right sink.
I saw chunks.
Of lamb.
They stopped
at the gate of the drain.

I shat thrice, mostly
water.
I was starving.

I ate a yogurt.

She put a slim box of tissues on the television table.

Which I moved to the mantle above the bed
so I
wouldn't have to
cup my little nose lettuces
in my palm
to then flick inside the toilet.

The lambs love me.
I know because when I pass they cry.
Their sweet little horns.
I shat water
and barfed with unusual force
because I ate myselves.
The next day I raised my ass in the air,
rolling from side to side on my thick king cloud bed.
I thought,
please don't let a fly
land upon my penis.

The lambs are in a square pen.
The area around the lamb pen
smells of the shit of lambs.

(add something here)

They moved my friends

into the chicken coop.
And where are the chickens?

I wished hard for them a larger pasture.

I wished the lambs a pasture the size of the donkeys'.
And I wished for the donkeys –
I wished something very large for the donkeys.

I am a donkey.

There was ginger ale, coke zero,
and Mexican beer
on the small cart of the small donkey.

The large and
heavy head of a
donkey
covered in several burlap sacks.

Okay so the lambs are just gone altogether now.

And so are the chickens.
And also the chicken pen has
opened up.
And when I said where are the chickens,
I had not looked
hard enough.
They were behind the lambs
where the laying happens.
I suppose the question was,
where are the roosters.

I mentioned the disappearance of the lambs to D. at lunch.
She did not care.
I am not going to speak of the lambs to ANYONE ELSE.

Alfred said: *are the dark trees at war with the darklike trees?*

People want to be scared.
And then you scare them.
I want to embarrass
you. To crouch
my stupid little swollen body.
It's getting longer.
Because I talk.
I rest
my hand on my own belly kindly
when I'm
being tender with myself.
The romance capable
only of girls
as girls.

I saw a photo of the orange frame
of your king bed.
Your waist is long.
And you have a bib of
sunburned skin.

A teak chair, palm trees, my folding lips.

Twenty-seven or eight thin trees rolling.

I can/can't leave the library again
to go and touch my pussy.

I found the sheep.

They're beside the donkeys.

The deeply unbuttoned, cruelly
white and crisp shirt he wore.
Fourteen being seven two times.
I know everything
I need to for the next 5 minutes.

The cacti have spikes and so
the cacti
are unsucked.

And one never knows where her
egg is
unless
you make a child
and the egg becomes somebody.

I've wanted to know which
clot or stream held my egg.

Silvergreen grass bushes
manicured with a decorative,
angular,
conspicuous artificiality –
It's attractive. It's very attractive.

At around 6:30 the birds chirp to annoyance

and then they sort of just stop.

I was on the bed reading Alfred.

Cinnamon
was sprinkled evenly over a great glass bowl of
chopped watermelon
on the evening
Toronto suffered a great flood.

They'll stop altogether absolutely as if conducted
and then just go again.
I can't
look it up because I don't care about birds.

The moon's in the day sky, peeking.

In fact, last night, very quickly, here,
on my cloud bed –
I heard the voice of a man.

I ate the apple the cop gave me.

My friend claimed to be driving with a crack
in his windshield
because
I was sick.
So
after we paid him off 50 dirhams
the cop gave me an apple.

The cop had an apple
and all cops have nipples
in the night.

The good and medium ass, the long and medium waist

of a man.

The bit of back fat that romances his crisp shirt.

I can wear a crisp shirt too and I have nipples too.

I have nipples in the night when I enter the café

and order a vegetarian meal

or chicken.

I have so much faith in the world.

I have so much faith in the cream of the world in its

spasms and cries.

I know what the world can do in an afternoon.

I know the sun excited –

slipping out the sky if he wants to

turn his light, a little.

I believe in the world.

And as I hold the hot and cold in hand

I could take my bra off and

put it back on again after.

One glass of wine.

One glass of spirits with citron soda.

One glass of spirits with cola soda.

One glass of wine.

One glass of wine.

Come and take down the motherfucking veil,

brother.

Let's be sisters in the night.

Let's be sisters in the night, brother.

One glass of spirits with the juice of a pregnant lemon.

I left mine on the table

when I retreated to the cabana

because

I don't like to be seen thinking.

I keep sensing this child

and love its length and red swimming trunks.
It screams the way I would if you
weren't inside me
as an idea to fruit or a
fruit to swallow.
As a line in a book I author
and you keep on your shelf –

I like very much that today I touched him.
It has a weight to it.
Creating a pulse and cave of my
lower abdomen.
Here
she is. I smell white guilt.

George wouldn't jump into the pool because of my proximity to his
father.
So I said, Hi George. George is two but
like, fuck George.
Also, he gave me cut-eye.

The half-circle watermark, like a rising sun, on the green bikini bottom
of his mother.

That I flattened my left hand into a star.

The corn your teeth kept.

The griot's songs

match the sky's
hard brightness,
and when he finishes
a silence sticks in my teeth.

In a Hello Kitty bathing suit, a girl.

I am completely uninjured.

It's 4:32.

Physical.

Full moon.

I could see everything at the pool.
I wasn't alone.
I wasn't physical.
I went upstairs and I was physical upstairs.
Then across the low cushion
my torso is a freshly-ironed
physical blouse.

A fountain before me flashes its wetness.
I lifted my shirt and doused my horns in it.
The water was physical in my intention.
You have to give the garden growth
there to balance out the sky
where light is blackness.

The intimacy between my index finger and the atmosphere
is physical.

"COME UP AND GET ME!"

I've been here.

This day has a look.

Earlier, I thought,

"I have to listen my whole life."

As I am certain and not.
Job never sinned from his lips. Job never sinned
of his teeth.

I want to cover my face in it.

And let it dry.
And tighten my skin.
And rinse it off.
And lather my face in it.
And rinse it off.
And lotion my face in it.
And emolliate my face in it.
And rub it in to sweetness.

I'm sorry I'm unsorry.
(No I'm not. I am physical.)

White pillows, two and four.
White pillows one and then four.
White sheets, cloud bed all white.
And unblank.
I am reading.

I didn't know where to place my excitement.
It's physical
and I gave it to aggression.

And of course the moon can strike you.

The night was bright enough that I wanted everything.
The night was bright such that the pool had transparency:
its visible grippy bottom.
We didn't need electric artificial light.
I left a man alone with a guitar.
I did something
I did something romantic in my room.
I went up to my room.
That kind of nocturnal light merited
event.
I probably also ate a Danone and loosened my bra straps.
This is speculation.
That evening is a night and I can't arrive in it.

Showering before dinner, wet hair at dinner, going to the gym.

He asked me if I was cold.

To make a work is to sit with your irrelevance

and confront your importance.
I mean, the swallows just fly.
And the papaya sweats when cut.
With the pad of my right index finger
I smooth my left brow.
It's so easy and feels
feels so physical.
The taste of plain yogurt
which has turned, slightly.

I knew I would change physically.

I have to report something physically important.

I have to report something physically uncomfortable.

I have to compose a list

until I am lifted up and turning, physically turning.

I fill the theatre.
It fills me aurally.

And then my beauty
meets me in fatty parts jostling.
I sort of control them.
As a unit
we make the natural noise of a
circumstance location and time.

I like mango.

Fertilized by a hot drink's exuberance,

the moon when it strikes

gets me physical and
important.

I said No, but I have to tell you – it's 'cause of physical reasons.

The inside of which is sticky.

A meeting point.

You know – *physical.*

I saw the stars

and I came after them.

They are

many raisins.

This is what I will say.

I physically got what I wanted.

Experiencing my return to a prior interest (unnecessary comma)
I realize how uninteresting
of a shape a
spiral is:

your blessed life
lying against your stupid life.

Attending an event in which you can
guarantee admiration
and then suffering that admiration ignobly.
Almost ignoring it.
As if it is the natural physical constant circumstance of your life
unlike
the longing for it physically.

I would like to be a shepherd of baby donkeys.

The shrubs like
very tight curls on the head of a boy.

I am ya okay
wanting to barf now. Physically all over every time.

As it's been I am
the pencilling sister.
From cloud to river to cloud.
Your sharp inhale,
communicating.

This here
distinct, physical medium mountain and physical medical log clouds;
bush, space, bush,
donkey. It's not
getting any less.
I will let it work on me physically.

He held his chin
and a great deal of skin
gathered in folds.
Bright blue blazer making
touch with a shock of
white hair.
Looking
like what one is is unavoidable and information
and physical.

I can't get back to the same physical place the same

physical location.

I decided that I was going to be
all the time.
A book tells me anything.
A book tells me
the person who
I will
get to
tonight maybe.

I could eat that, not go, not try, ok, fine.
Look.
I know that because of you
in part and
also because of Alfred.

I guess what I've done

is establish a goal
and approximated the
behaviour I believed
indicated its arrival.
Also I slander.
People
they see everything; they're blind.
Fuck marry kill.

A piece of couscous on his chin.

There are no more emergencies.

You have
dandruff and grey
and I
a white cap of emollients,
a goat on a cushion
my ass shrinking
with leisure.
Before me, in the name of seafood,
an insect bore the name shrimp.
It smelled like from where it came.
I resented its
singleness.
Oil pressed from the shit of sheep.
And the truth is it's an Israeli company.
I have to look up Zion and
I have to
buy a loofah.

And wasn't she a
cat for Christmas
last week?

Physical green cushion, with black physical stripes.

Physical circular stair
case.

Forcing a blush out of them.

Helps me understand
shame

as a social apparatus

so I just swam.
And feel so nice.

I said to Mohamed,
You've got your soul
patch on today.

The low part of the sky
slowly plumping with French.

The roof which condoms the sun from my face.
But I want to be black.
It's the birding hour.

I lick my lips.

A force transpires
when blood pools at my pussy.
A wild donkey,
behemoth head.

Both of us are wearing
our bathrobes outside.

Two things are sad in this light.

The black hole of your
sweat stain.

I put on my $300 bathing suit
to swim the cold waters.
To see it.

Six flies
host the white and king
cloud office
which itself hosts my succor.

I think you could ask your life for me. Sorry – for
more.

He said, You're from Africa?

Yes.
Which country?
Canada.

So far, I'm not that good at it.

I pulled intimacy
from my imagination and
presented it
as if
cocreated.

Maybe I should really eat a fruit.

Hi/bye.

He asked me,
Are you open?
I thought his meaning
was lost in the third language.
But no he meant are you open.

Like how the right side of my right upper neck side,
it has a lot of feelings.

Neon red
dragonflies
a foot above the pool
    skating.

They are leaving.

Physically when they are gone,
they will be
not here.

I
I was in a location and shifting.

I knew something.

It's physical and I didn't care.

You have a spider crawling on your collar.
Here – I killed it.

The rules of the sky in this village encourage it:
birds, little birds
fly in and.
And make a lot of noise settling –
I'm reading a terrible essay
on the Boston Review ok
and then they
shit on the way out.

A very little bit.

I am getting physical
about being.
I want to
purchase the night well
and haricots verts.
Every day every day haricots verts haricots verts.

Stuff.
Megagasm.
Mercy fuck.
Pleasure activist.

A shepherd of baby asses.

Okay I'm waiting.

The meat that made a meal

you have to physically kill a lamb

to put together that.

Can I haz

cream sauce.

The beau man points his peak eyes at you and you

don't want to cry.

Everything is happening.

Don't be sick in it.

The image crawls across the screen in a straight line like a battalion
   advancing.

God help me as I practice looking.

God help my intelligence as I employ it.

I have been shining.

The sun.

Our sun.

There's the residue of a burning and then
there are the goods of the
patisserie.

The daring whites of his lower goatee.

The crisp smile that might live forever.

I really don't want any questions.

These will lead to thinking.

I really don't want any thinking.

Thinking itself is not bare.

A five-month-old child as a gift.

To thinkers for their unintelligence.

You look at the pieces

and organize them by colour.

I haven't seen anybody

in thirty and one-four minutes.

Also,
I am sorry that I hate you because you hate me

because I hurt you because you hurt me because you are human in a
way that
disturbs me to the extent you strategize differently

than I do for a similar lack.

Inasmuch as our circumstances differ, yours being better.

Out of habit and fashion

I am merely talking.

I enter the restaurant. I want to know where to sit.

His beautiful wife. I said give her a kiss for me.

He said, Where, on the asshole? pursing.
No, I said.
North of there.

That laugh that we made
before the British people came.

There are chemicals.

When you're assessing my

location in a room.

Like the last time I got flowered I was fed.

That's frantic.

And he, he could spread his arms out, turn around and around, and say,
Look.

My œuvre

fits in my purse. I'm tired.

Of pretending I'm tired of pretend.

Being

neither like flowers

nor babies.

You can tell but it wasn't.

You can share; you're a liar.

You can tell and you can share; your lonely dream is potent.

There were no questions. It was all answer.

I answer my answer with answer and.

And. And. And.

Okay I skimmed the book; that's enough.

I skimmed the book; I looked at its photos.

I looked at its photos and saw that half the book was notes and biblio data.

Good being useful only for

the lookingness of a person's face torso, hands or teeth.

The skinny men have large physical hands here of muscle.

I haz long physical hands of length.

His money looks like simple paper.

My money like a small package.

His money looks like simple paper.

My money like a kept promise.

His money looks like mine in coins.

Found money having the rounded cheeks of grace.

Like

comfort and activity.

I like to think of my body as a garment.

I have borrowed my body.

It means I need all afternoon to think every day.

That's what it means.

It means money looks like movement.

I have to think about existence every fucking day.

And I am unwasteful.

If I don't consider the day how can I live in it.

I see the contents of the day I see instruments of the moment.

Often these are physical objects.

Often these are trees, and bushes, and bushes
and trees.

I consider the objects in the day.

I consider the distances between bodies.

If I am the same as other people, why don't they like poetry. I love
poetry.

If I am the same as other people, why don't they like poetry. I love
poetry.

And I am the same as other people. I've checked.

Sometimes I watch a video and feel good that I am the same as
other people.

Like I am certain I am seeing myself

in the faces of the five boy children crowded around the library computer.

Headlines. He like headlines.

You like to get to the logic.

You both put sprinkles all over everything.

He wants to sell me something I've already purchased.

You want me to like

something I already love.

I understand that facilitating a pleasure is distinct from
being responsible for it.

This is how I'd guess
that in sex you like to please.

Some men know about women.

I am frightened of these men

a little

and relieved

when a man knows something about women.

When a man knows something about women.

Men who know about women understand there aren't

any.

This is me washing my thong panties in a pistachio-coloured basin.

I am totally undisgusted by your dandruff.

Me getting my nipples pinched by the bar.

It's natural, he said.

It's definitely physical.

The tight waist of my grey jeans. Jeans I consider light black.

I consider my jeans "light black."

They are reaching towards blackness.

How would you know?

I wanted to say how (the fuck) would you know?

The piece of foil covering the breakfast tray blows to the side.

He let me see

the invitation and then he took it back.

The first time their person is before your person.

I read the invitation

and then I gave it back.

I understand that things are as they are and to prefer them otherwise is wasteful.

I am unwasteful.

I do not prefer that you are other than you are.

I do not prefer that I am anything.

I do not prefer the neatness my imagination offers the future.

I do not prefer the tidy offering my imagination gives the future in the form of fantasy.

I will not prefer in this manner at all.

When I shorten my breath so that I can extend physically.

I have seen small noises when I shorten my breath physically to extend what I created.

I'm sad about a thing I willed myself to have no attachment to.

Physically I suppose I'm human.

Physically.

I am undemocratic.

I said hullo and then retreated.

A man wanted praise; I used the word interesting.

On page 28 the author discusses intoxication.

We have the sickness of incense.
May God heal us.

That sounds good in English.

This sounds good in Arabic

to my

Anglo-ass ears:

Gnawa blitu-nah. Gnawa blitu-nah.

I see the words "middle-class neighbourhood" and put the book down.

A lily

bloomed in my chest.

Grew to the base of my throat.

The women singers beating their drums in a tight circle – physical

excellence. They were unsorry.

I didn't tell you I gave in and held back.

I didn't tell you I danced in the late afternoon light and was scared.

When you moved towards me.

There are four turtles now in one of the herb gardens in the restaurant.

They keep escaping.

Someone puts them back.

I am watching one climb the short fence right now.

He is succeeding.

She is succeeding.

It has succeeded.

The sound of its hard belly hitting the ceramic

was like a rock dropping.

Walking down the stairs loudly,

each new awareness
constituting event

that then has to get translated
physically, so I march.

At dinner you wore a beautiful sweatshirt.

You looked beautiful at dinner.

You looked handsome at dinner.

Your sweatshirt was navy.

You looked handsome and clean-pressed at dinner;
in the morning you looked fresh and handsome.

The proprietor doesn't want to stop in the day
less in the night so does he tarry.

I have tarried all day

turning

to knowledge for comfort.

For the function of knowledge is such.

Every day I can eat an egg and not suffer.

From the ingestion of the egg to be specific.

This is my human lot.

Tomorrow I will tarry though yea my heart is without hate.

My simple heart.

I have not wanted to state its requests.

Knowing is a consequence of believing.

And I would like to have better belief such that I could know better were I to engage in that.

If I were interested in knowing then I should be better in belief.

Most all our actions incohere.

I might be a turtle but not entirely.

Their hard shells colliding. I'm not sure if it was a fight

or a fuck.

His delight is in the law of the Lord and on this law doth he meditate day and night.

The ungodly are like the chaff which the wind driveth away.

Ya Aish – why do they have to be perfect?

They don't have to be perfect, but I would like that they are good, in the heart.

Anahata deficiency excess.

Anahata excess deficiency.

I would like to move.

Move.

I would like to move.

I'm gone.

I am composed of 6 children

including a grandmother.

When I smooth my brow it comforts the little boys inside me.

At a large meeting table

are the little children I carry.

There's Plum and slash

teenaged Sadie.

There are the triplets who are eight

and

then there is Joe.

The wound returns in ritual guise

leaking song and dance.

The ceremony gives the wound a voice.

The ceremony blows.

This time

the body

is in

vuln'rable.

The wound. The wound. It jamais fully disappears.

The need for the ceremony, perennial.

I'm just as bad as him.

I don't want to

show my wound.

The initial wound, indelible.

I'm just as bad as him.

The wound defines community.

We have the sickness

of jawi. *May God*

heal us.

The trance gave me space.

The trance released me.
I am going to make some space
for my head.
I am going to make some space for my head.
I'm going to travel.

The other one in his quilted sweater looked as good on this day as any other. I am pleased

to gaze upon his large and fantastic head.

The way I look is very good. I have to exalt.

And move quickly.

I was a queen in the night

beneath mascara flakes

I might have dreamed of a goat.

All of us are men and I am too.

What am I going to

do about myself.

The tree is branching.
And the repose has lifted.
And the honeyed moon has waned.
I think I am working as a worker.
I am weary
at the future.
I am always interested in things; it will never stop.
I can plump minutes with my always interest.
But I am weary.

The throat.

Thy throat.

Thy throat is

comely.

I'm going back.

See ya I'm going back.

To make a crown

that you can speak.

And wear in your memory.

She said to imagine a column extending from the

top of my head and to climb it.

Grace and reality acquaint

through the senses. And thus.

I left already.

I wasn't there already.

I put mustard on the yellow chicken.

And on each and every fry.

I am leaving. Bye.

Good

bye I have to part.

I left.

Only an emotion remains

which has taken over my right hand fingers.

Which has taken over my left hand fingers and

keeps my buttocks fixed.

Going completely physical.

I should have said no.

I should have said absolutely not:

I'm working.

Girliness is a North American affectation

that none of the women here

are sick with.

May God heal us.

Today it was today I thought of the smooth cheek skin and aquiline nose of a person.

In the morning I had a belief in her.

I had other beliefs this morning I did not express.

And I lost the doctrine that my dreams provided me with,

this morning.

I wet my sheath

with mineral water and imagination.

I have a neck. It's Monday. I have a neck.

I'm still friendly.

If I shift my posture perhaps my right hand smaller fingers

will

unnumb

or whatever.

My hands.

My fingers my hands.

I raise them.

I am standing.

I exalt.

Which brings sensations.

Let's sing.

Let us sing:

May we be healed may we be comforted.

May we bathe

in waters sweet of our enoughness.

May we after anoint in the sweet oil of our enoughness.

Cinnamon and cloves, lavender and myrrh, exalt.

May our enoughness as bounty please us.

May our enoughness, the bounty, please us.

May we know and move in it.

May we know and walk as it

in the blue hour dawn morning, the bright light of noon and after,
the blue hour at dusk, the handsome navy that is night, and the blackest
truth in a moonless sky, may we know, may we be pleased, may we
exalt!

Marvin said he listened to my voice letter as he

fell sleeping and thus my voice as if from a cloud
and I was so calm and naked with fatigue 'cause I'm an animal.
I just slapped a wasp and put its stinger in my palm.
Good-
looking men will
white clot you with knowledge. There are
three Rubenesque British women here today.

The day is ordinary and beautiful.

I am ordinary and beautiful.
I am the day.
The day is in its afternoon.
I am in my afternoon.
My jiggling butt in this dress.
I have
100 dirhams in my right bra cup.
I want to tell you something.
The griot took a break and then he rebegan
wearing pointy dress shoes in the
West African and Italian style. He is
in the afternoon.
And I'm sitting right behind him.
The sun is so hard in its afternoon sky.
The waitress with the very large and happy butt passed by.
I love her giant smile.
It's creative.

There are three of us.
I am talking about physical typing as in chucka chucka cha
and backspacing
in this physical semi-desert
my nose pores don't fill with oil.
I am as good-looking as I want in the late dawn, my nose pores empty.
I still scrubbed; when I had
nothing to scrub I continued. I'm alright.
I'm as I can be I'm not wet or anything.
I haven't been cut.
Where did you go in your short pants, your small legs.
Where did you go?
I am so interesting in the afternoon.
Where now indeed it is late.
Hi, everybody.
Let's haz a cheeseburger.

[4:28:08 p.m.] asj: hi love i'm working with others near I cant talk
[4:28:15 p.m.] asj: but I love you & all your ways & every look you have
[4:28:22 p.m.] asj: youre incredible. youre tall
[4:28:24 p.m.] asj: I like tall
[4:28:28 p.m.] asj: DO YOU HEAR ME?
[4:28:32 p.m.] asj: where are you in the afternoon
[4:28:37 p.m.] asj: are you in the afternoon
[4:28:42 p.m.] asj: are you the afternoon are you the light
[4:28:54 p.m.] asj: are you a link in the website of my butthole

This particular physical ingestion experience has provided me no lens.

I am as ordinary in my thinking as always.

Nay, perhaps I am more so

for I reach not

into the stomach of my mind

for that half-chewed image

for which to surprise a you whom I imagine as the part of me

that lives in others.

For there is an Aisha in some

bodies

which allows them to be pleased

in what I am pleased in.

And the amount of Aisha

you hold is a product of

our locations relative to each other

in terms of which organs our

minds (ow!) perform.

I said I had a stomach in my

head; that's true.

I didn't eat your bonbon

because I didn't really want to.

I just sort of wanted to.

And that isn't reason enough

to eat the second

of two fine bonbons

of a friend you have with a very

tall and hard and soft body

such that you might regret

the calculation in child-likeness you

made, successfully, in order to

hug him, because now having

felt his perfect and able

man of a body

well you want all or more of it

than the short time

provided by a calculated gesture.

If you are seen

you are not unlike

everybody.

Everybody makes moves.

Everybody is socialized to calculate.

People become holy people in order to

escape power play

and well, good for them.

I have to participate.

I have to participate.

Crying my face in the night of the lightless theatre.

I have to cry if I don't I will flirt myself to self-harm.

His body is totally alright.

It's fine.

Like as fine as

broad shoulders are interesting.

I have excitement. I hope today I'm great-looking.

It is earlier in the afternoon.

And windy.

I have everything to do as I want in the afternoon.

You have a good time and I have a good time.

And everyone looks everywhere.

Everyone looks everywhere and thinks: okay,

what should I do now?

I've seen everyone do that

every time.

Baraka said, Who say you gunk ugly and they

the goodlookingest?

Each line living its entire life

because
I'm not going to suffer excellence
by lending her my intelligence right now.
The palm trees, the bamboo bush.

The red and green long-leaved bush,
the tall grass –
all dancing.
The bamboos
prostrate and rise
in mourning
every day they do that.

I went to Brazil three years ago or four years ago.
I don't even know when I went to Brazil.
A long man was there.
I spoke to him under the shade of narrow leaves.
Lying on cement he touched my knee, I liked it, he told me I should
listen. This
gave me feelings
of
a four-year degree.

I haven't told you anything stupid yet.
I'm working up to it.
I have enough days to form a hard crust around my
face of you which you then can
break out of and tell me questions.

Remember when you said that thing
and I responded?

There was falling and no bottom

and I wasn't even
dreaming. I am talking about a
ten-hour train ride up the vein of a country.
This is why I have to
beat the floor
and squeeze it tightly with my senses.
My back loves the floor and my butt.
My thighs love the floor and my heels.
The back of my head and my palms.
If I roll it's so more of me can touch the more.
If I lift it's to know the floor at a point
with greater intensity.
All my thighs, they know to know the floor
is to lie upon it.
Is to pinch and squeeze.
The closeness of the ground to the air.
It's
incredibly close.
The ground and the air are incredibly close.

They talked about me in Arabic but
I understand the word "Canada."

There are no specifics.

It's obvious.

They look good, they look bad, I would
have sex with them, me too.

There are several types of strangers.

Strangers who take photographs.

Strangers who smile too
readily (these are the worst)

and strangers who reveal the fact of your
own strangeness
somewhere else.

The moment when you understand

a city won't seep inside you.

You were in its old part
making a long enough love.

Everybody loves the old part of every city.

Do you love the new part.
Of a city who it is becoming?
As you walk it.

You have to love the future of a city to love a city.
It is the opposite of loving a man.

I am to take my first right, my
second left.

I translate the map into imperatives.

I don't understand pictures – seriously.
I bought an ugly sweater at the Tangier flea market
violet as are all sweaters ugly.

Then for twice its price
I bought a dirty scarf
with white crescents on it,
a scarf of seeing
to protect my good head
from evil except
it is much too
big and hot.

The trick to haggling is leaving.

Nobody
nobody else would buy that purple sweater.
I didn't even buy it.

One of the little children within me
reached to my
tight light black jean pocket
and offered the vendor a coin.

Everybody looks from far enough away like a person.

The way they move.

So many people are human.

The sun of Tangier is blue, and white, and clean.

It is the sun why they stayed here.
The sun here is also an ocean and also a sea.

I don't care about Paul Bowles seriously.

He took my phone and he touched my sleek cellular phone.
He didn't ask and I didn't ask either
when I gave my phone
back to me.

Sharing cabs makes the most sense ever
since citizens are not strangers.

The point is it's not my country.

The waves came toward me like
hope.

The intimacy of the beach
destabilizing.

The waves.
I wanted to flee softly.

The world is a body.

Young men wear track suits all over a country.

Still, I saw athletic training
in these selfsame suits.
On the beach. It is the blue hour.
I write as I walk the waved cement
boardwalk

in bright gold sleeves.
Or else my brain will
shit itself.

The little children cup their
small and warm, their
soft little hands
over the mouths of each of their contrarians.
This is what happens inside when I'm
weeping.

A low
cement wall.
Perched by six
late-teen girls.

Tangier at the blue hour.

Somehow I know what I am.

The bartender hates everything.
Including her black blazer
within which she's still cold.
She hates
my hair,
my stupid question,
my girlish tone, that I
went outside and
came back in. (We're in Le Coeur de Tanger.)
She's fixing her blazer in the mirror.
Un mélange, she said.
I
asked who came there
to have an excuse to speak.

Freddie Mercury's beautiful fuck
teeth.

Deluxe Essentials.

I want to talk about
why I won't take photos:

I'm greedy.

Charcoal sidewalks, gently
destroyed and softly littered.

If leisure is the dress of a city,
it is found on the body
of the city's men.

Rod Stewart.
In a three-piece beige suit
sucking
so hard.
And I am a professional exalter.

Oh brie a German song.

My lips are dry and I'm alive.

Something deep fried and fishy and
soft and wet and fishy inside.
Tell me, little children, what
is the difference
between experience and event.

Barry White's eyes
are physically tiny.
My dry lips being
physically dry.

But then Michael Jackson.
Whose sex
is secret
from the viewer
in that he shows it.

Koch wrote about Hide Life.
That was one train. I wasn't there.
Ariana
wrote about Hide Life and I was:
something popped
within me cool and blue.

For a second I had a
worry.

The snake can't fucking tell
its tail from its prey.

My own little children
also have swallowed each other.

If you move one train,
there might be another behind
so I'm looking.

The red was violet.

"It's a pleasure,"
he says
when I laugh at him because I like it.

I like how you've done actually.

I like how honest and
enthusiastic you are in moments.

I like the lively way you live.

How they are.

How a person should be is how they are amen.

Every position has its weakness.

I like

how you are

which is why

I am you.

What we do is we're all
naturally intelligent.

We are all naturally intelligent.

People are interested in succeeding at existence.

We have different
concerns to accommodate. Wet your lips.

Seeing the sea tells me something about the future.

I promised my children we would sit quietly

so I could host their quarrels and recovery.

It's physical,
the line between murder and kill.

That birds fly. One.

A bunch of birds, three, several
birds, what the fuck.

What happens.

Do they enjoy it?

People they want to arrive

and arrive and arrive.

I am a cyclist in the night.

In the morn; moreover I am eyes.

I can be eyes in the night when I'm lonely.

I can tell you about yesterday;

it was everything. I touched a stuffed camel.

I touched

a stuffed stork sporting a fez.

I had fine fish in fine company; I spoke voluminously, in English, I talked, thinking.

I was a flower in the morning.

I need to go see my sisters and frères.

"Black Africa" "Black Africa" "Black Africa" "Black Africa"

In the bubble of nonbelonging like a room you can do a lot of things in

there such as

let your face out

briefly.

When I come inside and into Canadian belonging are people boring or weird I dunno.

I return to a place I've rested; the politeness conventions injure.

The Britishness, the sheer secret Britishness of French people.

More things did I walk into.

Such as small hot churros in my mouth oh Lord.

More things I did enter such as swordfish and fries oh Lord.

Tangier,

oh Lord.

Something bad happened to me once.

I had a knowing I

didn't make action of.

Now why I did not make action of this knowing has a long story which ends with the little children within me having fought their most viciously.

Send her to the fracture clinic she did na do nothing.

Vous êtes prets?

D'accord.

A dead sperm whale.

The camera aimed at its chin and belly.

A figure in fluorescent orange, a man with
blue gloves.
You don't see the gloves until he runs.
Because the whale's abdomen explodes and
whale innards vault into the right
side of the screen. I see a three-foot liver.
The sound is wet.

I didn't write this I think I told it

to men.

I said I understand that here the women
don't perform girliness like for instance for extreme
example Japan but in Toronto Ontario Canada
it is a thing to
cover your power in pink
and just rest there not scaring yourself and certainly
no one else.

A story can be only one part.

Observing is all the analysis needed by anyone.

I have to let the city give.

I haven't figured out yet
how much
a person should eat at a breakfast buffet.

I have lived 12 thousand days.

I went upstairs.
I considered flying.

Frenchness is merely

Britishness with a dab of
butter and
two winks.

My marvellous children.

My light-filled house.

My charming husband.

My air-filled home.

Cats very close to my window cried
and then
fought and then
were silent like popsicles. There were two
cats out there and certainly also
a human baby.

How does it feel?

People come up to the mountain to get their coolness.

Everybody needs the coast and goes there to get hurt by waves.

They don't stop and they will absolutely not.
Everybody in the mountains getting hugged
by rock.
Everybody inside waiting for the face to dry.
Everybody's shorn head wet with what else.

Every greedy living cat crying as a wind for the middle ear.
Do you hear me?

Everybody makes things
or provides services.
Some people at the fact of their birth
accomplished their service.
There are a lot more people like this than you basically think.
Some people keep busy to
put quotes around their essential birth service.
Basically,
I could leave the hostel room if
the morning wouldn't pass my face and
demand of it a poem.

**Can't believe I'm saying this but
I gave too much of my left body to the sun.**

And now the shadow of my injury is with me like a chill.

Is that you running up the stairs?

It's after lunch on Saturday.

I went to your office and I found your office
unharmed by your presence.

It was so boring I just left.

Months and days.

The afternoon and the night.

I am telling you I ate a lot of produce at lunch on a Saturday.

I can't tell it's Saturday

so I'm uneasy physically.

I'm not sure if I tried to say something sisterly and failed or if I
put a cut in the air
to keep our wound alive.

I misestimated your recovery

on a Saturday
which feels so unlike itself
I don't want to do anything for a few hours
but focus on getting
a Saturday feeling.
It hurts. I have to say –
it hurts.

I could watch a movie. I just don't feel Saturday enough to keep going.

I gave myself a gift by getting my feet black this morning at the bequest
of the sun this morning on the hammock in my insistence.

Do you have insistence?
I have 14 reasons in the night.
And 7 seriously right now fly familiars. Crawling with their
complicated colour.
A fly was physically on my thigh.
I get fed
because I like time
enough to disciple in it.
There are 7 flies walking upon The Book of Questions.
These flies show very good taste
but they need me only because
I put food all over anything I carry.
The flies know all about me.
They're always
rubbing together their hands.
It's compulsive.
Oh my —

a fly just tried to
hump
its brother
on my pillow.

Everybody has so many minutes and
what do they do with all of them?

Food takes up a lot of people's minutes.

That's okay : food's okay.

It's hateful

to think of the people as losing

because I'm sorry the people

the people win.

What I mean is you can't take the juice out of the life of

everybody even if he is sick

with the blanket which

covered the final days of Ivan Ilyich.

That's not nice and this isn't getting any Saturdayer.

All these flies like tiny, stupid

OCD lions.

One is moving along the floor like a snake.

Holding my front neck with

my left hand physically to read
O'Hara.

I can and will and can and will and stop.

When I place the violets
of my hand to keep myself sure in the neck
it speaks to a future
I won't lend myself now –
it's too late.
I've already chosen a sort of
rarified present tense as a mode
of operating.

I took the back path to get to the library from my room.
I climbed a short fence of a hill that was buttoned in cacti.
Two boys and a girl of three on the other side of the wall
laughing
at me.
So I waved.

The limpness of a bird's legs in flight.

The place, the question, the question.

The place, the interest, the question.

There is the place.
There is what you do in the place.
There is your belief.
There is the faith in a knowing.
There is your instruction
by the gods.
There is your instruction as you are told.
There is your relief.
There is your disquiet.
There is your encounter.
That was it there.
Your encounter in the night.
Or before a flippant and loud
late afternoon sky.
A giant stone toe at the site of an ancient oracle.

There is the place.
What do you turn your face to in the name of instruction?
When you follow what the bells arrange
for the afternoon air
when you keep going
you're laying on your path surprise
because the dress you are wearing is destiny
and you can like that or you can not like that.
I am talking about
will.

Everything matters and is nothing.

Ringlets carved in stone. Very physical.

Speaking of lambs I am one.

Speaking of lambs I am a sheep. Baaa. Kill me.
Speaking of lambs I am a sheep.
I clip into the vestibule
two little sweet horns
I clip into the vestibule
because I am cloven.
I clip into the vestibule and right away
I die 'cause I'm a sheep
and rise again as a sort of
long-necked bird.
I sort of die before you
and later we eat
my sheep body
as a tajine with prunes
or a couscous.
I am the distant hiding meat
you can get to after
you have eaten the beads of
wheat that surround me,
wheat beads that are the soil
in which I am buried
because I'm dead again.

The book of you

Today I account for yesterday.

Yesterday I would have accounted for the day before.
I didn't write yesterday.

Yesterday was Friday.
Thursday was the seventeenth; I'm using love as a sieve.

I went to the college and I taught the children.

Then,
because a girl on chat roulette
said she'd
patronize a jazz club were she in Toronto
and we believe in signs
diddly wat dit dit dat
neither of us finished our beers.
Walking home with powdered donuts in my pocket.

Who are you
to me
tonight, Black History Month?

Because our oneness forms a filter

that sifts
out untruth
which then hangs between the cellular strings
that join our airs like
spittle
stretched long between the tongue and the teeth.

Somebody asked me about you.

I asked me about you. I was
in Boulder on a twin bed
under an ankle-length
red dress both brilliant and matte.

I hung it there to block the light,
and so that I'd bleed.
(I did.)

Ava said that if you look up into the dress it
was an ocean and diaphanous.
I haven't looked into the dress yet. I'm saving that.

I asked myself about you.
I asked myself about you.
I want to lift you slash
throw you to the clouds.

I'm saving that.

I am above the clouds.

I am now passing through a cloud.

I see a cloud the size of a Honda Civic.

In which you come here bearing wine and brie

and we suck on each other's bodies for life.

It's four o'clock.

It's four o'clock. I'll play

a beautiful woman plucking a coarse hair.

It's three a.m.

The yoke that is sun
leaks from my eye sides
what I did was
go into your purple

and take a swath of velvet but
I DON'T NEED ANYONE ELSE'S FUCKING VELVET-

-I've seen the truth.

She looks like a man.
She's elderly, 80-plus.
The colour of wet sand, she has a chandelier of
wine-coloured
I-don't-know-what's hanging behind her chin
like a bubbly beard.

She looks angry.

A dream in which I wore a black wool skirt with pleats

of the sort that
the insides
of the pleats were of the same fabric but red
and in movement, yes, the red was revealed:
a vaginal skirt.
And I am very happy.

I play air

with my body.

I play
time across my body and power.

When you look at me being seen you will witness a forward power

as it's true
whenever I consider power I think about my arms and their infinitude.

The healer said I was very angry.

What happened is I fell.

Neck-high into a pocket –
and then got fed
lines made of block letters
and that smelled like paint.

On Bloor were two bike cops

Black and at least one
was beautiful.
The other wore a
balaclava.
We noisily didn't acknowledge each other.
And the pretty one
was painfully well-groomed
and the other one
had too much air in his pants
where his bum could have been
not that I like
too much ass
on a man
still,
I looked at their guns.
The wind blew one's notepad down.

That's it.

I didn't want to go so I didn't go.

I did want to post something online so I posted something.
I wanted to conceal and confuse so I did.
I wanted to cover and also to reveal and so I did.
I do believe
this is a beginning.

If you sift
and then gather the dirt into a line, you have a story.
You can put perfume on that line but I'm not
anymore a liar.
I want to smell the armpits of the line

like how the unit of a poem
is your mouth.

The end.

I just wanted to say
there's no salvation here.

Just a gap
between what I am and what it was
thought I am
it
wasn't understood
and now I understand
that it wasn't understood
and I'm lonely.

Book – you're no more a friend than my thighs.

And I have all these conversations with various yous
and in them I explicate my position
and cement it really
which is not –
it's not grace.

And I don't want to
talk about my plans my intentions my plans or
hold up my plans to any scrutiny or better them or
read up about you more
to try to learn your choreography like
as if I am not so subtle elegant and of grace as I am now
in this bold blue sweater of my 2nd best friend
as the caffeine energizes my spectrum
and the colour of the sky slaps me in a sexual way.
I think about the whole length of the day
and where in it I can inject a joy deep into its tissue.

Do you tire of me?
Should I abandon you?
Am I holding too
closely unto your neck?
Have I been a
greedy one and
noisy?
Have I been very noisy
and you suffer in a
quiet way with
secret
and I have suffered also too in this way maybe
grace is to let our suffering
take a walk
and be seen with all its regions showing.
My flat ass
and
beautiful decisions
are calling me.
Are you going to call me?
I
can do everything today.
If I wear the loveliest tights from Winners
I can bike and never be killed.
I can prompt
the sacking of oppressors
and not be
revenged upon,
have a high fat snack and then
soar as
is my duty.

I never thought – and I don't care I just never
thought, "Toronto."
Never.

I can tell you
anything.
As I hold up my blouse
and show you
my world.
I can give you everything
and together we'll advance
for the hot hope of you
getting actual
and me
getting actual too.

I'm sleepy.

"Purple in her womb or
dark in her bosom or
dark in her lap
or
violets in her bosom"

I guess I just
wanted to
come here.
Yeah.
I wanted to come here –
because
it is nice here.

I wanted to tell you some secrets.
I want a different relationship to my stories.
I said I am cold and tired of where I have been as a supplicant
when I am here and north and bourgeois, they'll eat a
better dinner than I will eat but
I also will tonight in my sweet dress, my eyeballs filled with roses,
dance.
I will dance.
And in this way I am extending
and I'm not interested in comparison because I can basically
not give a shit I mean I've got five, six senses and then there's
the whole blue universe
like
the sound of a hard crust collapsing
the baguette as it's torn
it and the other noises that have
wet my ear lately the
tinkle
the violet tinkle of the nail spa alarm system
and the hard and unhopeful scrapes of their chairs
my sisters, my brothers, of the food court
the ignoble scrape of the metal would
ruin me except
I can't be ruined.

What time is it?

I hope you come here with your rented car.

You're not coming.
And I can't have you this evening.
I have to put the flowers around my
own throat.
And buy myself a film.
The plush seats
will be the violets of my lap.
I'm going to begin now
anointing myself with the oil of
your absence. That is this book.
And I made the book of you
in your absence
and I'll come into the house
and in the hot oil of your absence
my anointment
is a rose-shaped burn
at my crown.
I'll buy me flowers and cover my chest
protecting my health in violets. I can't stop.
But I can have this open
and we might
communion then
right among the spaces
between
my side and arm and your
arm and side
and your thick
torso
and behind that your
tight heart
and the space between that nut and
some energy around which there is no space.
We dip dates into a good wine
and have communion.
Have we the same
mouth?

Sometimes.

I'm right on top and over Miami.

A rust-coloured substance covering the water
like
mold and gross and woah

palm trees,
a golf course,
fellas
in pink jersey fabric.

I see a grey rash of townhomes.

I see tarmac, and good.
GOOD.

I stood on a violet stool and I looked deep

into above for a moon:
I had a lunacy.

The mites of my unswept floor attacked my ankles.
I bathed with a furor.
I anointed my soft with the
butter of nuts
I was sodden.

Not sodden I was sweet
for I danced
in the sharp light
of my lunacy and the shapes I made
O O O
I had
geometry.

Here I am it's Monday.

I wrote it as that, Monday.

And you are

in my eyes.

I have this amount and I want to give it

to this

little flat surface.

Reader, that I put a kiss on your face in the middle.

That I lifted my shirt that
beside the bar or tabernacle
I raised my warm hand
into your shirt and
we were delighted.
Reader that I've had you
that you've
known me.

I will walk two three blocks down the street in you

and purchase with a toonie hot from my backside a baguette.
Rubbing the butter on the ripped open inside
as if the baguette is an armpit.
I'll hold the bread to your face
and look to see if your chin remains as you chew.
You smell
like sour watermelon.

What doesn't happen in a year happens in a day.

In your house apartment condominium mansion flat.
Because I know you have an oil there.
I want you to put
your finest oil
into the finest
small open-faced container you have
yes and I want you to bring
this oil
to the body of a soul you love
and I want
I want you to anoint
the brow
of the body
in this oil
in your love.
                    Selah

As if one morning, after breakfast, someone asked you,

"What do you want to be when you grow up?"
and for three years
you just kept belching.

When you were

out for dinner with your boyfriend
'cause you have one
or
at the Eaton Centre
buying tops
with your money
'cause you have some
I was here
with my iMac
putting my body on a line.

'Cause I have to.

Though I'm
dizzy now.

I went upstairs
to see what you had for my eating
and to show you my toenails
which I painted myself
poorly
because I'm not good at
things like neatness
and
when I lay my body down you called
and we chatted because it
nourishes us
and then you called
and we chatted
because it is water for me or milk
talking to you
and I ate an egg
sautéed in
organic garlic
and I lay my body
back down
and I was
feeling fat and small
but then a line burst onto me
and so I came home to it the computer and
now
again
I'm dizzy.

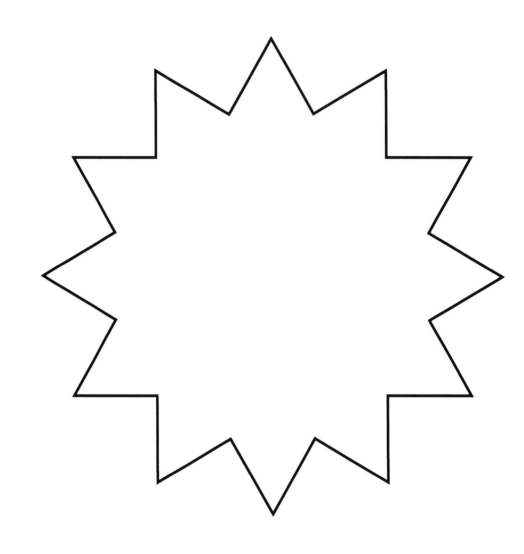

My fever broke.

It is a burgundy day.

I spent my exuberance on dance this afternoon

so page
what I've left for you
is quiet.

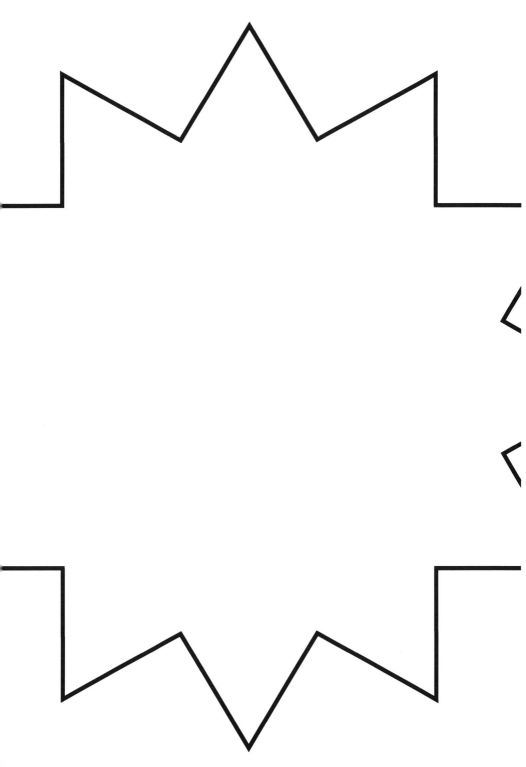